VOCAL SELECTIONS
FROM
THE MOST HAPPY FELLA

By
FRANK LOESSER

Contents

	Page
BIG D	15
DON'T CRY	24
JOEY, JOEY, JOEY	6
MY HEART IS SO FULL OF YOU	27
SOMEBODY, SOMEWHERE	30
STANDING ON THE CORNER	3
THE MOST HAPPY FELLA	18
WARM ALL OVER	12

Applications for performance of this work, whether legitimate, stock,
amateur, or foreign, should be addressed to:
MUSIC THEATRE INTERNATIONAL
545 Eighth Avenue
New York, NY 10018
(212)868-6668

A Publication of
MPL COMMUNICATIONS, INC.

EXCLUSIVELY DISTRIBUTED BY

HAL•LEONARD®
CORPORATION
7777 W. BLUEMOUND RD. P.O. BOX 13819 MILWAUKEE, WI 53213

Standing On The Corner

By FRANK LOESSER

Excerpt from Act I Scene II of "THE MOST HAPPY FELLA"

Joey, Joey, Joey

By FRANK LOESSER

Tex - as av - o - ca - do _____ Or may - be Ar - i - zo - na sug - ar beet. _____

The wind blows in _____ And she

sings to me, 'cause I'm one of her ram - blin' kin. _____ She sings,

L.H.

Jo - ey, _____ Jo - ey, Jo - ey _____ Jo - ey, _____

mp

9

10

Warm All Over

By FRANK LOESSER

Ev-'ry - time you smile you get me Warm All O - ver.

Some-times I feel kind of out in the cold, But then I

touch your hand _____ and I'm home   home a - gain And

Warm   All   O - ver,   Warm   All   O - ver,

Gone are all the clouds that used to swarm all o - ver.

Please al - ways let me keep feel - ing the way I do, So

Warm All O - ver with a ten - der love for

you.

Big D

By FRANK LOESSER

I mean Big D, lit-tle a, dou-ble l - a - s.

And that spells Dal - las, My
that spells Dal - las, Where
that spells Dal - las, Just
that spells Dal - las, I

dar - lin', dar - lin' Dal - las, Don't it give you pleas-ure to con-
ev - 'ry home's a pal - ace 'Cause the set - tlers set - tle for no
dig a toe in Dal - las And there's oil all o - ver your ad -
mean it with no mal - ice But the rest of Tex - as looks a

fess _____ That you're from Big D? My, oh
less _____ Hoo - ray for Big D, My, oh
dress _____ Back home in Big D, My, oh
mess _____ When you're from Big D, My, oh

Excerpt from Act I Scene II of "THE MOST HAPPY FELLA"

The Most Happy Fella

By FRANK LOESSER

Most Hap-py Fel-la   In the whole Na-pa

Val-ley _____ In the whole Na-pa Val-ley, The

most hap-py man _____ That's me!

Sentimentally

In the win-ter time ____ from 'Fris-co

mf

She was-a write to me _____ one post - card.

Then I was-a write, then she was-a write,

then I was-a write, then she was-a write, then me, then she, then

me, then she, and now _____ She's-a bring ___ the

spring - time fast! She's - a make the green come

on — the vine! She's - a send me _____ her

pho - to - graph And she was ask - in' - a me ___ for

mine. I'm The Most Hap - py Fel - la

(With great vigor)

f (ben marcato)

Excerpt from Act I Scene IV of "THE MOST HAPPY FELLA"

Don't Cry

By FRANK LOESSER

weep ___ Come on back ___ in the house, lit-tle sheep ___ Come on

back in the house for a smile of wel-come and go to

sleep. Yes, I know how you feel, It's that wild run a-way feel-ing

poco accel.

in your heart _____ When you've had the wrong dream, ___

cresc. poco a poco

And you wake with a start. Well, Don't

Cry Don't Cry Come on back in the house and don't

a tempo

cry Come on back in the house and get out from un-der that

old cold sky and Don't Cry.

rit

My Heart Is So Full Of You

By FRANK LOESSER

You, so full of you._____ There is no room _____ for an-y-thing more.____

mf animato ma non troppo   *cresc.*

What oth-er wish can I wish? What oth-er plan can I plan?

What oth-er dream can I dream, and what for?__ What-ev-er for? When

Somebody, Somewhere

By FRANK LOESSER

Wants lone-ly me to smile _____ and say hel-

lo _____ Some-bod-y, Some-where _____

wants me and needs me _____ And that's ver-y won-der-ful _____ to

know. _____